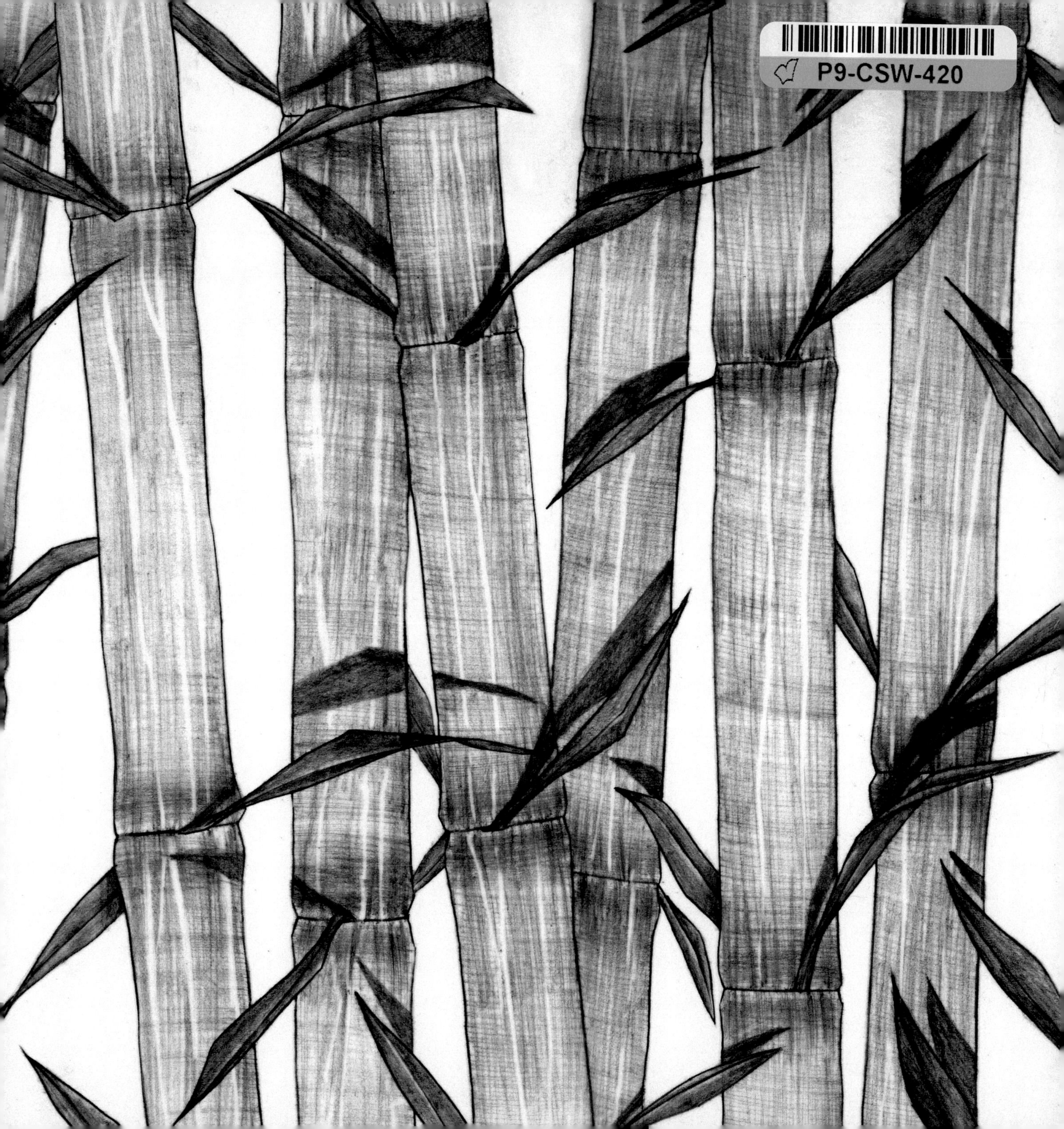

ISBN-10: 1482379953
ISBN-13: 978-1482379952

To

EMILYN, FOR THE LOVE AND SUPPORT

KAYA, FOR THE INSPIRATION

~ R.M.Y

JacJac

AND THE

Lucky Bamboo Stalk

STORY AND ILLUSTRATIONS BY R. MARK YGONA

Not long ago, there was once a young girl named Jacquelyn who lived in the city.

Each summer, Jacquelyn's parents sent her to visit her grandparents' farm in a land far, far away.

SPLASH!

On the farm, she loved to run across the open fields and play with the farm animals.

DURIAN

CACAO

MANGO

BREADFRUIT

BANANA

CHICO

LANSONES

TAMARIND

COCONUT

GUAVA

But her favorite thing to do was climb the trees that grew on the farm. Often she would play well into the early evening hours until Grandma called her in for supper.

"Jacquelyn, suppertime!" Grandma would call out, but there was no answer. Again, Grandma called out, "Jacquelyn, suppertime!"

Finally, Jacquelyn replied, "I'm coming, Grandma!" She climbed down from a nearby fruit tree, and ran towards the house.

Grandma shook her head and said, "From now on, I'm going to call you 'JacJac' so that I can call you twice by just saying your name only once." Jacquelyn giggled with delight at her new nickname and went inside to wash up for supper.

The next morning, at the crack of dawn, the rooster crowed three times.

The warm rays of the morning sun poked through the bedroom window waking JacJac up. After breakfast, JacJac helped Grandpa with farm chores.

As the sun rose higher and higher, the day got hotter and hotter. It was by far the longest drought in three years.

Grandpa decided that he would not be tilling the fields this season with Narra, his water buffalo that pulled the plow. There would be no seeds to sow. It was time to take Narra to the village market in hopes of trading him for food and supplies that would last them through the drought.

"GRANDPA, LET ME BRING NARRA TO THE MARKET WHILE YOU TAKE YOUR AFTERNOON NAP," SUGGESTED JACJAC.

"OKAY, BUT MAKE SURE YOU MAKE A FAIR TRADE," AGREED GRANDPA.

GRANDPA PLACED HIS STRAW HAT ON JACJAC'S HEAD TO KEEP HER COOL UNDER THE HOT MIDDAY SUN. JACJAC CLIMBED ATOP NARRA, AND OFF SHE WENT.

On her way to the village market, JacJac met a shaman. The shaman was on his way to the market too. He had come down from the nearby mountain to trade herbs and trinkets for fruits and vegetables that he could not grow on the rocky mountain soil.

THE SHAMAN WAVED TO JACJAC AND ASKED, "OFF TO THE VILLAGE MARKET, I SEE?"

"YES, I'M TRADING GRANDPA'S WATER BUFFALO FOR SOME RATIONS THAT WILL LAST US THROUGH THIS DROUGHT," REPLIED JACJAC.

THE SHAMAN NODDED AND SAID, "YES, THIS DRY SPELL SEEMS TO BE ANOTHER SPOT OF BAD LUCK THAT WE ARE ALL HAVING LATELY. I LOST MY PET EAGLE RECENTLY JUST ABOUT THE TIME WHEN ALL OF THE VILLAGE'S MUSIC WENT SILENT. WELL, MAYBE I CAN OFFER A LITTLE BIT OF CHEER. HOW ABOUT I SAVE YOU THE TRIP TO THE MARKET AND TRADE YOUR WATER BUFFALO FOR A LUCKY BAMBOO PLANT?" THE SHAMAN PULLED OUT A COCONUT FROM HIS SATCHEL AND CRACKED IT OPEN WITH A MACHETE. HE DROPPED WHAT LOOKED LIKE THREE SMALL PEBBLES INTO ONE OF THE HALF SHELLS. SUDDENLY, JACJAC'S EYES BEAMED AS A TINY BAMBOO PLANT MAGICALLY SPROUTED IN A CURLICUE FASHION.

"YES, LET'S TRADE," SAID JACJAC AND OFF SHE WENT RUNNING BACK TO THE FARM.

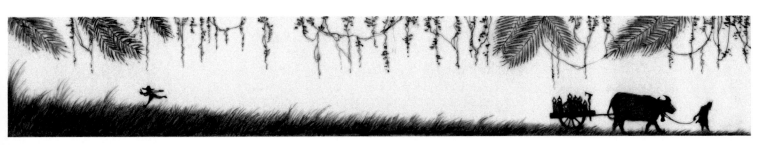

BACK AT THE FARM, JACJAC SHOWED OFF THE BAMBOO PLANT TO HER GRANDPARENTS. HOWEVER, THERE WAS ONLY SADNESS IN THEIR EYES.

GRANDPA SIGHED, "JACJAC, I HAD ASKED YOU TO MAKE A FAIR TRADE FOR NARRA. THIS PLANT CANNOT PROVIDE US WITH FOOD AND SUPPLIES TO LAST US THROUGH THE DROUGHT."

GRANDMA CHIMED IN, "JACJAC, HAVE YOUR SUPPER NOW, AND THEN GO STRAIGHT TO BED. TOMORROW, GRANDPA WILL GO TO THE VILLAGE MARKET AND TRADE SOME OF HIS TOOLS FOR RATIONS."

AFTER SUPPER, JACJAC BROUGHT THE BAMBOO PLANT INTO HER BEDROOM. SHE STARED AT IT FOR A MOMENT HOPING THAT SOMETHING MAGICAL WOULD HAPPEN AGAIN AS IT DID EARLIER THAT DAY. THEN, MAYBE GRANDPA AND GRANDMA WOULD BELIEVE HER. BUT NOTHING HAPPENED. DISAPPOINTED, JACJAC PLACED THE BAMBOO PLANT ON THE WINDOW SILL BEFORE GOING TO BED. LATER THAT NIGHT, A GUST OF WIND SWEPT THROUGH THE VALLEY KNOCKING DOWN THE BAMBOO PLANT OFF THE WINDOW SILL. JACJAC WAS TOO SOUND ASLEEP TO HEAR THE COCONUT SHELL HIT THE GROUND BELOW AND SHATTER INTO PIECES.

THE NEXT MORNING, AT THE CRACK OF DAWN, THE ROOSTER CROWED THREE TIMES. JACJAC AWOKE TO DARKNESS EXCEPT FOR A FEW STRANDS OF SUNLIGHT STREAMING ACROSS HER BEDROOM. JACJAC SAW THAT HER BAMBOO PLANT WAS NO LONGER SITTING ON THE WINDOW SILL. INSTEAD, SHE FOUND HERSELF STARING AT A GIANT BAMBOO STALK!

JacJac raced out the door to find her grandparents already outside. They were scratching their heads as to what they were seeing. Amongst the grove was a single giant bamboo stalk that grew higher than their eyes could see.

Before her grandparents could stop her, JacJac began to climb the bamboo stalk until she could no longer hear their pleas for her to come back down.

Finally, JacJac made it to the very top.

AT THE TOP OF THE BAMBOO STALK, JACJAC DISCOVERED AN OLD MANSION BUILT WITHIN THE WEB OF BRANCHES AND ROOTS OF AN OLD BANYAN TREE.

CURIOUS AS TO WHO LIVED THERE, JACJAC FOLLOWED THE GIANT STEPS THAT WERE CARVED INTO THE BANYAN TREE'S ROOTS. WHEN SHE FINALLY REACHED THE MANSION'S DOOR, SHE KNOCKED UNTIL THE CARETAKER OPENED THE DOOR. HE HAD POOR EYESIGHT AND HAD TO SQUINT HIS EYES TO NOTICE JACJAC. HE FINALLY SAID, "HELLO THERE, AND WHAT BRINGS YOU TO MY MASTER'S DOORSTEP?"

JACJAC REPLIED, "SIR, WOULD YOU HAPPEN TO HAVE SOME FOOD TO SPARE AS MY FAMILY'S RATIONS HAVE RUN OUT?"

THE CARETAKER GLANCED OVER HIS SHOULDER AND SAID, "ALRIGHT, BUT YOU MUST HURRY AS MY MASTER, THE ENCHANTRESS, DOES NOT LIKE VISITORS ESPECIALLY CHILDREN LIKE YOURSELF."

IN THE KITCHEN, JACJAC WAS SERVED A LARGE SLICE OF CUSTARD PIE. EVERYTHING INSIDE THE MANSION SEEMED FIT FOR A GIANT.

JACJAC WAS JUST FINISHING THE LAST MORSEL WHEN SUDDENLY AN EERIE HISSING SOUND CAME FROM UPSTAIRS.

THE CARETAKER WHISPERED, "QUICKLY, YOU MUST HIDE! THE ENCHANTRESS MUST NOT SEE YOU."

IN THE CORNER OF THE KITCHEN, THERE WERE CLAY WATER JUGS. JACJAC CLIMBED INSIDE AN EMPTY ONE AND HID QUIETLY.

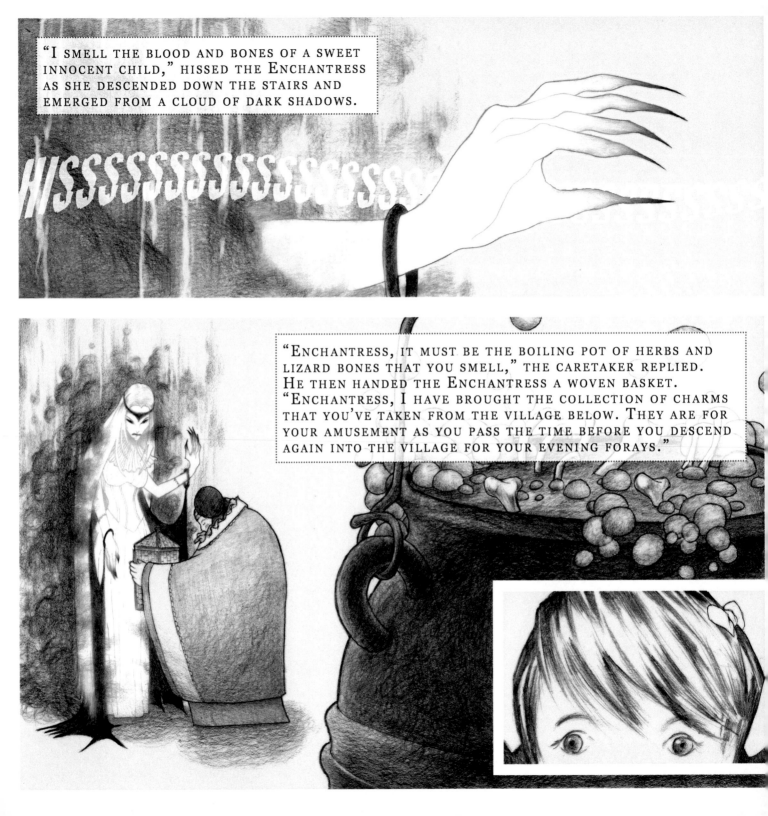

"I SMELL THE BLOOD AND BONES OF A SWEET INNOCENT CHILD," HISSED THE ENCHANTRESS AS SHE DESCENDED DOWN THE STAIRS AND EMERGED FROM A CLOUD OF DARK SHADOWS.

HISSSSSSSSSSSSSSSSSS

"ENCHANTRESS, IT MUST BE THE BOILING POT OF HERBS AND LIZARD BONES THAT YOU SMELL," THE CARETAKER REPLIED. HE THEN HANDED THE ENCHANTRESS A WOVEN BASKET. "ENCHANTRESS, I HAVE BROUGHT THE COLLECTION OF CHARMS THAT YOU'VE TAKEN FROM THE VILLAGE BELOW. THEY ARE FOR YOUR AMUSEMENT AS YOU PASS THE TIME BEFORE YOU DESCEND AGAIN INTO THE VILLAGE FOR YOUR EVENING FORAYS."

HISSSSSSSS SSSSSSSSS

CURIOUS AS TO WHAT THE ENCHANTRESS LOOKED LIKE, JACJAC PEERED OVER THE LIP OF THE WATER JUG. WHAT SHE SAW SENT CHILLS UP AND DOWN HER SPINE. THE ENCHANTRESS WORE A CAPE THAT WAS BLACK AS NIGHT. HER LONG FLOWING WHITE ROBE MATCHED BOTH HER PALE COMPLEXION AND LONG SILVERY WHITE HAIR. IN STARK CONTRAST TO HER SEEMINGLY AGELESS APPEARANCE, THE ENCHANTRESS HAD SEARING BLACK EYES AND TEETH LIKE THOSE OF A FERAL BEAST.

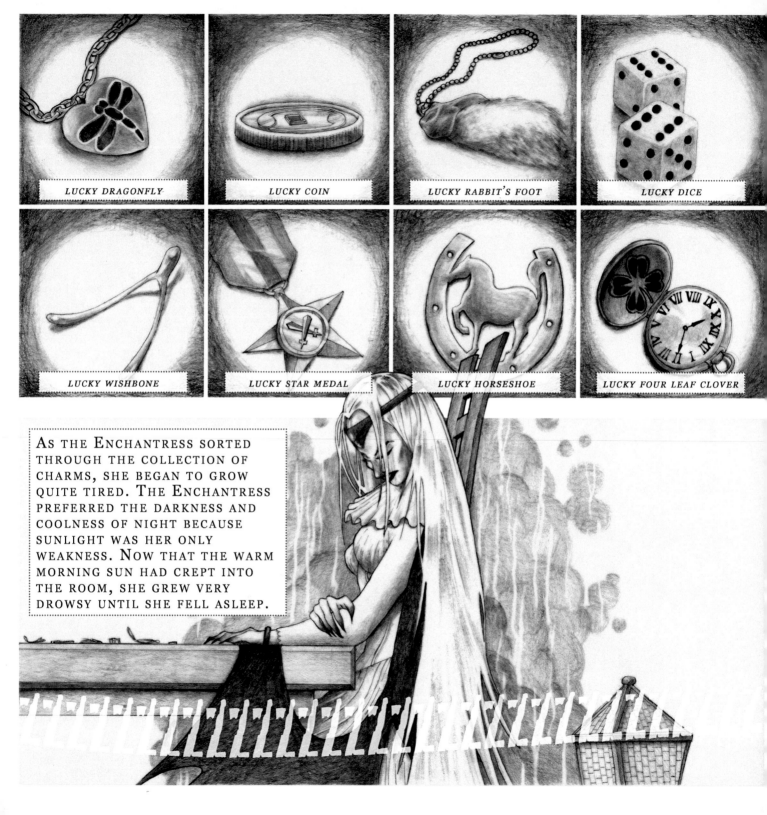

LUCKY DRAGONFLY

LUCKY COIN

LUCKY RABBIT'S FOOT

LUCKY DICE

LUCKY WISHBONE

LUCKY STAR MEDAL

LUCKY HORSESHOE

LUCKY FOUR LEAF CLOVER

As the Enchantress sorted through the collection of charms, she began to grow quite tired. The Enchantress preferred the darkness and coolness of night because sunlight was her only weakness. Now that the warm morning sun had crept into the room, she grew very drowsy until she fell asleep.

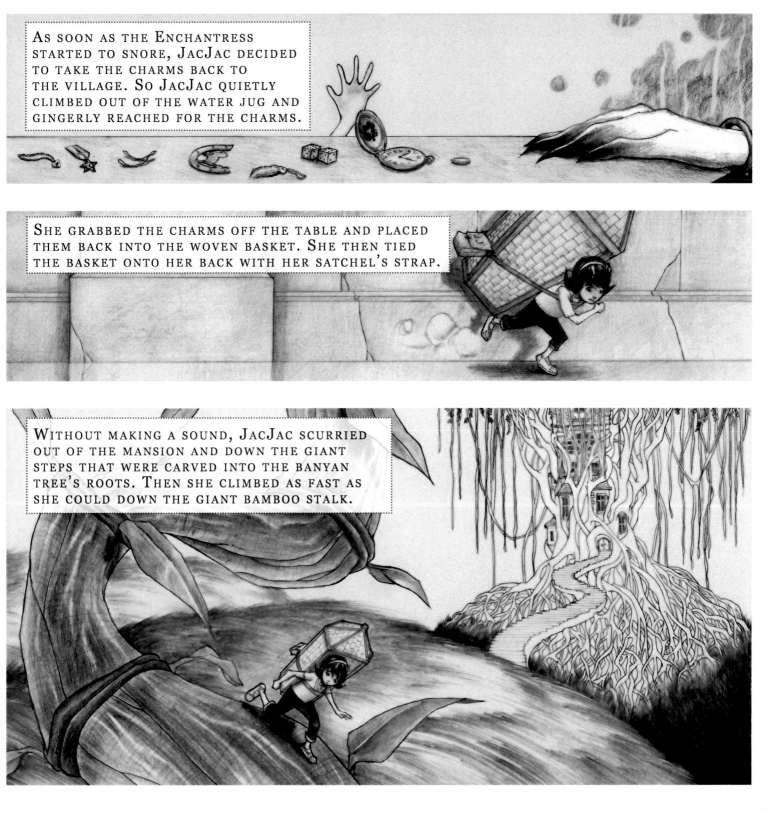

As soon as the Enchantress started to snore, JacJac decided to take the charms back to the village. So JacJac quietly climbed out of the water jug and gingerly reached for the charms.

She grabbed the charms off the table and placed them back into the woven basket. She then tied the basket onto her back with her satchel's strap.

Without making a sound, JacJac scurried out of the mansion and down the giant steps that were carved into the banyan tree's roots. Then she climbed as fast as she could down the giant bamboo stalk.

THE PEOPLE OF THE VILLAGE WERE JOYOUS TO HAVE THEIR LUCKY CHARMS BACK. TO SHOW THEIR GRATITUDE, EACH SHARED A SMALL PORTION OF THEIR RATIONS WITH JACJAC AND HER GRANDPARENTS.

NOW JACJAC AND HER GRANDPARENTS HAD ENOUGH RATIONS TO LAST THROUGH THE DROUGHT.

AFTER HEARING JACJAC TELL HER STORY OF HER MORNING ADVENTURE, GRANDPA DECIDED THAT IT WAS TIME TO CUT THE BAMBOO STALK DOWN BEFORE NIGHTFALL. HE WAS AFRAID THE ENCHANTRESS WOULD SEE THAT THE BAMBOO STALK CAME FROM THE VILLAGE BELOW AND SEEK REVENGE DURING THE MIDDLE OF THE NIGHT.

BEFORE GRANDPA COULD TAKE A SWING WITH HIS MACHETE, HE LOOKED UP TO SEE JACJAC CLIMBING UP THE BAMBOO STALK AGAIN. SHE WAS CURIOUS TO FIND OUT MORE ABOUT THIS MYSTERIOUS ENCHANTRESS. GRANDPA SHOUTED AFTER HER BUT TO NO AVAIL. JACJAC WAS TOO FAR UP TO HEAR.

At the mansion's door, JacJac gave a good knock.

The caretaker opened the door and said, "Hello there, and what brings you to my master's doorstep?"

JacJac replied, "Sir, would you happen to have some food to spare as my family's rations have run out?"

The caretaker thought this request sounded familiar and squinted his eyes as he studied JacJac. He finally said, "You look a lot like the young child that came here earlier this morning."

JacJac replied, "Sir, I believe that person you're describing ran past me just as I was coming up these steps."

The caretaker glanced over his shoulder and said, "Alright, but you must hurry as my master, the Enchantress, does not like visitors especially children like yourself."

IN THE KITCHEN, JACJAC WAS SERVED A GIANT CORN ON THE COB. JACJAC WAS JUST ABOUT TO TAKE ANOTHER BITE WHEN SUDDENLY AN EERIE HISSING SOUND CAME FROM UPSTAIRS.

THE CARETAKER WHISPERED, "QUICKLY, YOU MUST HIDE! THE ENCHANTRESS MUST NOT SEE YOU." JACJAC RAN OVER TO THE CLAY WATER JUGS AGAIN, BUT THIS TIME THEY WERE ALL FULL OF WATER. SO JACJAC HID BEHIND THE TALLEST ONE.

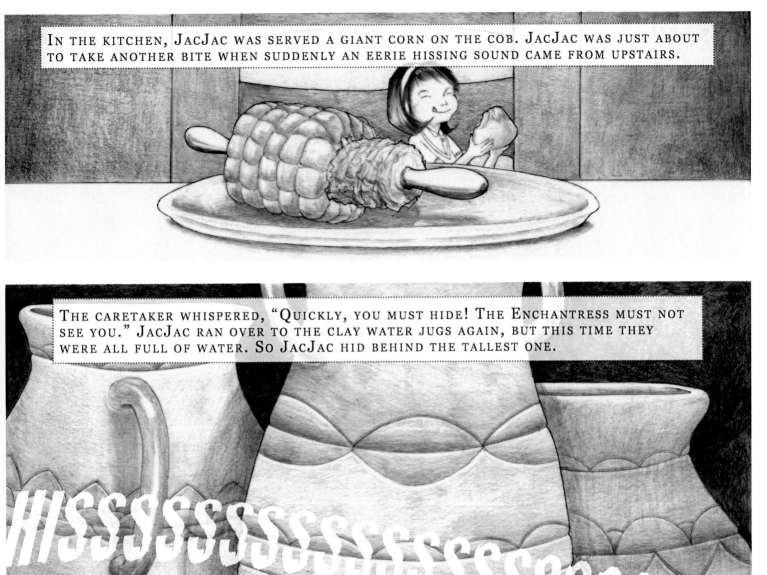

HISSSSSSSSSSSSSSSSSSSSSSSSSSSSSS

"I SMELL THE BLOOD AND BONES OF A SWEET INNOCENT CHILD," HISSED THE ENCHANTRESS AS SHE DESCENDED DOWN THE STAIRS AND EMERGED FROM A CLOUD OF DARK SHADOWS.

THE CARETAKER REPLIED, "ENCHANTRESS, IT MUST BE THE BOILING POT OF HERBS AND EYES OF NEWT THAT YOU SMELL." THE CARETAKER THEN WHEELED IN A LARGE COVERED BIRD CAGE. "ENCHANTRESS, I HAVE BROUGHT YOU THE GIANT EAGLE AS YOU REQUESTED."

The Enchantress replied, "Yes, I would like to pluck its feathers for a special spell, but for now I must return to my afternoon nap." The caretaker then left the room leaving the Enchantress to take her nap.

JACJAC THOUGHT THIS MUST BE THE PET EAGLE THAT THE SHAMAN HAD LOST. AS SOON AS THE ENCHANTRESS AGAIN DOSED OFF TO SLEEP, JACJAC CREPT TOWARDS THE CAGE AND BEGAN TO PUSH IT TOWARDS THE DOOR.

WITHOUT MAKING A SOUND, JACJAC SCURRIED OUT OF THE MANSION AND DOWN THE STEPS THAT WERE CARVED INTO THE BANYAN TREE'S ROOTS. THEN SHE CLIMBED AS FAST AS SHE COULD DOWN THE GIANT BAMBOO STALK.

ONCE AT THE FARM, JACJAC OPENED THE CAGE SETTING THE GIANT EAGLE FREE. GRANDPA WAS MORE THAN CONVINCED THAT HE MUST CUT THE BAMBOO STALK DOWN BEFORE NIGHTFALL. FOR SURE THE ENCHANTRESS WOULD SEEK REVENGE IF SHE DISCOVERED THAT THE BAMBOO STALK CAME FROM THE VILLAGE BELOW.

BUT BEFORE GRANDPA COULD TAKE HIS MACHETE OUT OF ITS SHEATH, HE LOOKED UP TO SEE JACJAC CLIMBING UP THE BAMBOO STALK AGAIN. JACJAC REMEMBERED THAT SHE HAD LEFT HER SATCHEL BACK AT THE MANSION. GRANDPA SHOUTED AFTER HER BUT TO NO AVAIL. JACJAC WAS TOO FAR UP TO HEAR HIM.

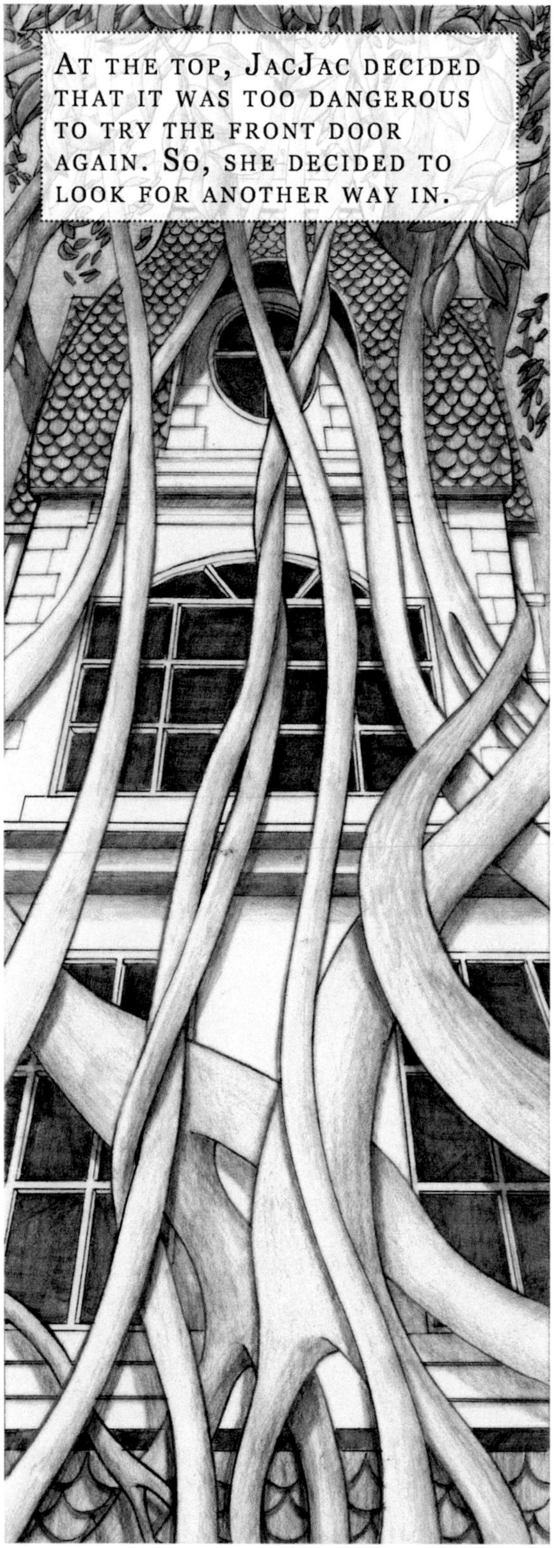
At the top, JacJac decided that it was too dangerous to try the front door again. So, she decided to look for another way in.

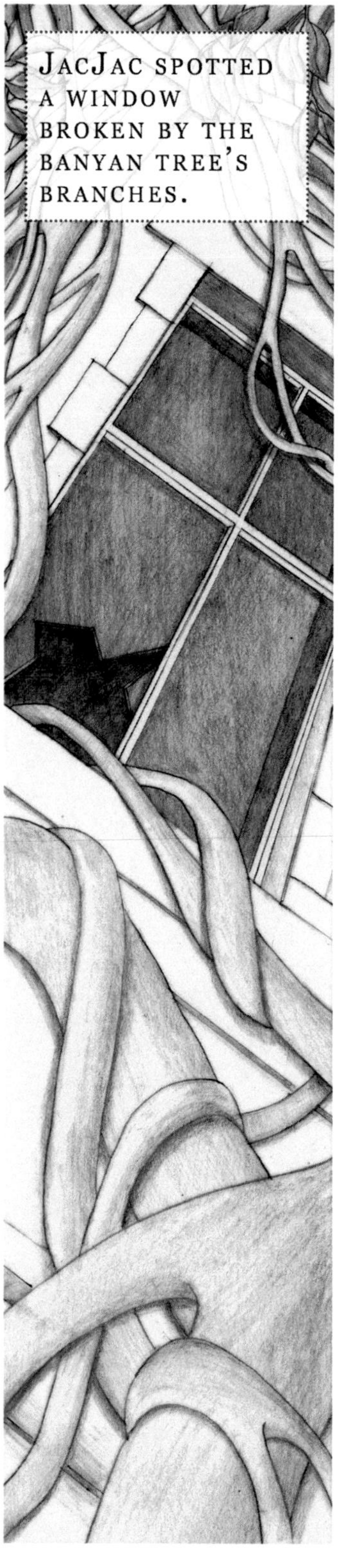
JacJac spotted a window broken by the banyan tree's branches.

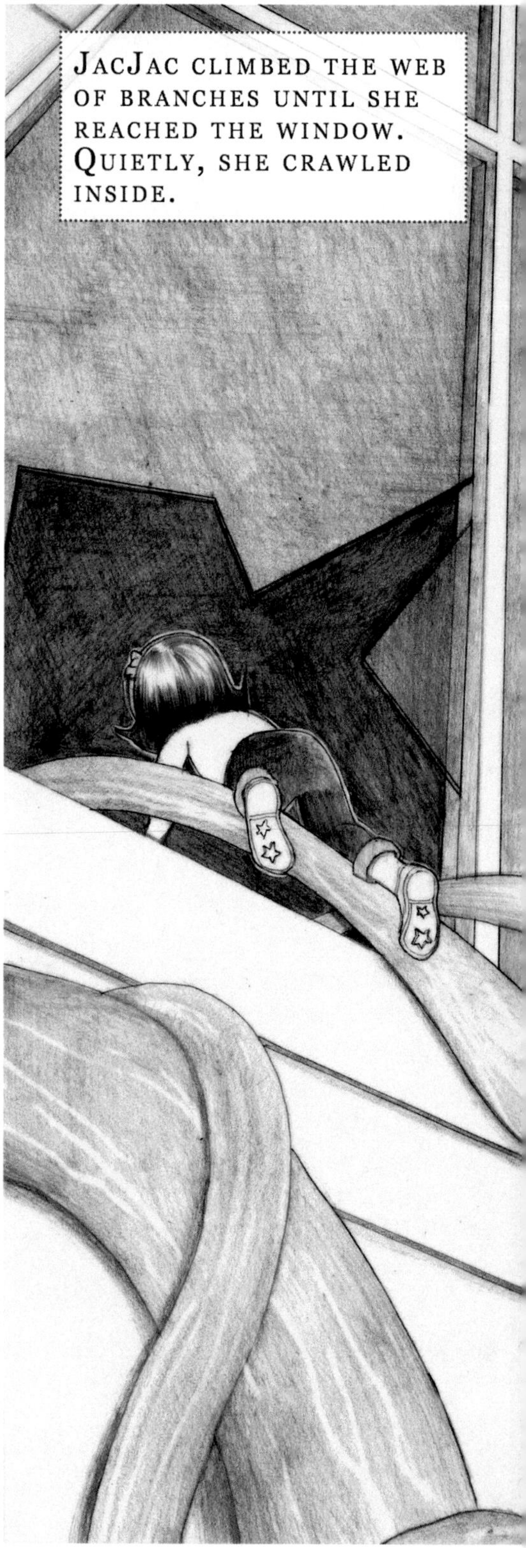
JacJac climbed the web of branches until she reached the window. Quietly, she crawled inside.

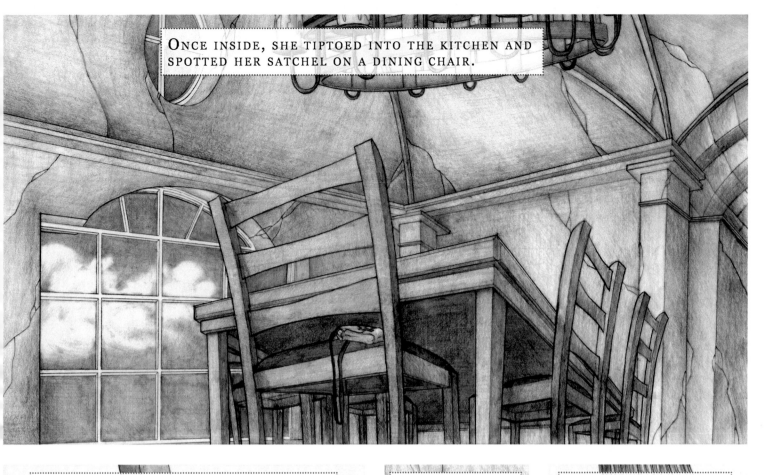

ONCE INSIDE, SHE TIPTOED INTO THE KITCHEN AND SPOTTED HER SATCHEL ON A DINING CHAIR.

JACJAC GRABBED IT, BUT BEFORE SHE COULD SNEAK OUT OF THE KITCHEN, SHE SUDDENLY HEARD THE NOW ALL TOO FAMILIAR EERIE HISSING SOUND COMING FROM UPSTAIRS. THE CLAY WATER JUGS WERE ON THE OTHER SIDE OF THE KITCHEN- TOO FAR FOR JACJAC TO RUN OVER THERE IN TIME.

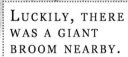

LUCKILY, THERE WAS A GIANT BROOM NEARBY.

IT WAS MADE FROM THE STEMS OF DRIED COCONUT LEAVES. IT WAS TALL ENOUGH FOR JACJAC TO HIDE BEHIND.

"I SMELL THE BLOOD AND BONES OF A SWEET INNOCENT CHILD," HISSED THE ENCHANTRESS AS SHE DESCENDED DOWN THE STAIRS AND EMERGED FROM A CLOUD OF DARK SHADOWS.

HISSS SSSSSSSS

THE CARETAKER SAID, "ENCHANTRESS, I AM SORRY, BUT YES, THERE HAS BEEN A YOUNG GIRL WHO HAS TRICKED ME INTO INVITING HER IN. IF SHE IS HERE, SHE MAY BE HIDING IN ONE OF THE WATER JUGS."

THE ENCHANTRESS AND CARETAKER PEERED INTO EACH CLAY WATER JUG, BUT JACJAC WAS NOWHERE TO BE FOUND. THINKING THAT THEY MUST HAVE BEEN MISTAKEN, THE ENCHANTRESS AND THE CARETAKER LEFT THE KITCHEN TO PREPARE SPELLS.

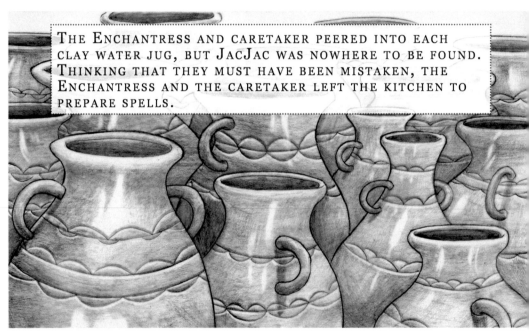

WHILE HIDING IN THE SHADOWS, JACJAC FOLLOWED THEM SILENTLY INTO A SPECIAL ROOM CALLED THE CHAMBER OF SPELLS.

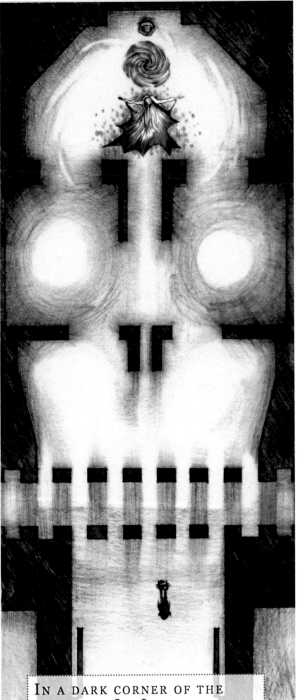

IN A DARK CORNER OF THE CHAMBER, JACJAC DISCOVERED THE MUSICAL INSTRUMENTS THAT WENT MISSING FROM THE VILLAGE.

AMONG THEM WAS GRANDPA'S OLD GUITAR. JACJAC WENT TO RETRIEVE IT.

HOWEVER, JACJAC TRIPPED.

BONK! CLANG! CRASH!

THE INSTRUMENTS MADE A HUGE CLATTER. THE ENCHANTRESS SAW JACJAC. SHE HISSED AND CHASED AFTER HER.

JACJAC GRABBED THE GUITAR AND RAN.

THE ENCHANTRESS WAS NOT AS FAST AS JACJAC WHO WAS NOW FAR DOWN THE BAMBOO STALK.

JACJAC SAW GRANDPA BELOW AND SHOUTED FOR HIM TO START CHOPPING DOWN THE BAMBOO STALK.

AS JACJAC SAFELY JUMPED OFF THE BAMBOO STALK, GRANDPA BEGAN TO HACK AT THE BAMBOO STALK WITH HIS MACHETE. THE BAMBOO STALK SHOOK AND SWAYED BACK AND FORTH WITH EACH SWING OF THE MACHETE.

SOON ENOUGH, THE BAMBOO STALK BEGAN TO FALL. BY NOW, THE ENCHANTRESS WAS WEAK UNDER THE HOT AFTERNOON SUN. IT WAS BURNING HER SKIN. ALL OF A SUDDEN, SHE LOST HER FOOTING, SLIPPED AND FELL OFF THE BAMBOO STALK.

THWARCKKK!

THE ENCHANTRESS BURST INTO FLAMES UNTIL ONLY A CLOUD OF SHADOWS WAS LEFT.

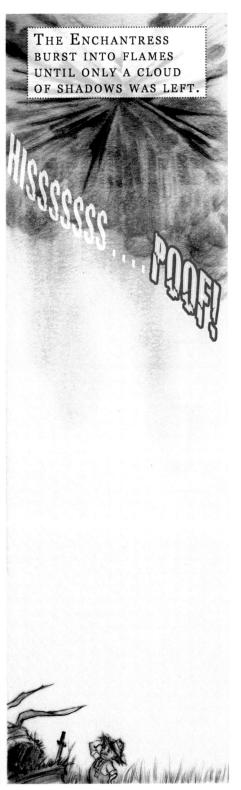

HISSSSSSS ..... POOF!

SEEING THAT THE ENCHANTRESS WAS GONE, GRANDPA AND GRANDMA RUSHED TO HUG JACJAC. THEY WERE HAPPY THAT SHE WAS SAFELY BACK WITH THEM AT THE FARM.

GRANDPA'S EYES LIT UP WHEN HE SAW HIS GUITAR, FOR IT WAS THE SAME GUITAR HE SERENADED GRANDMA WITH MANY EVENINGS AGO.

CLICK!

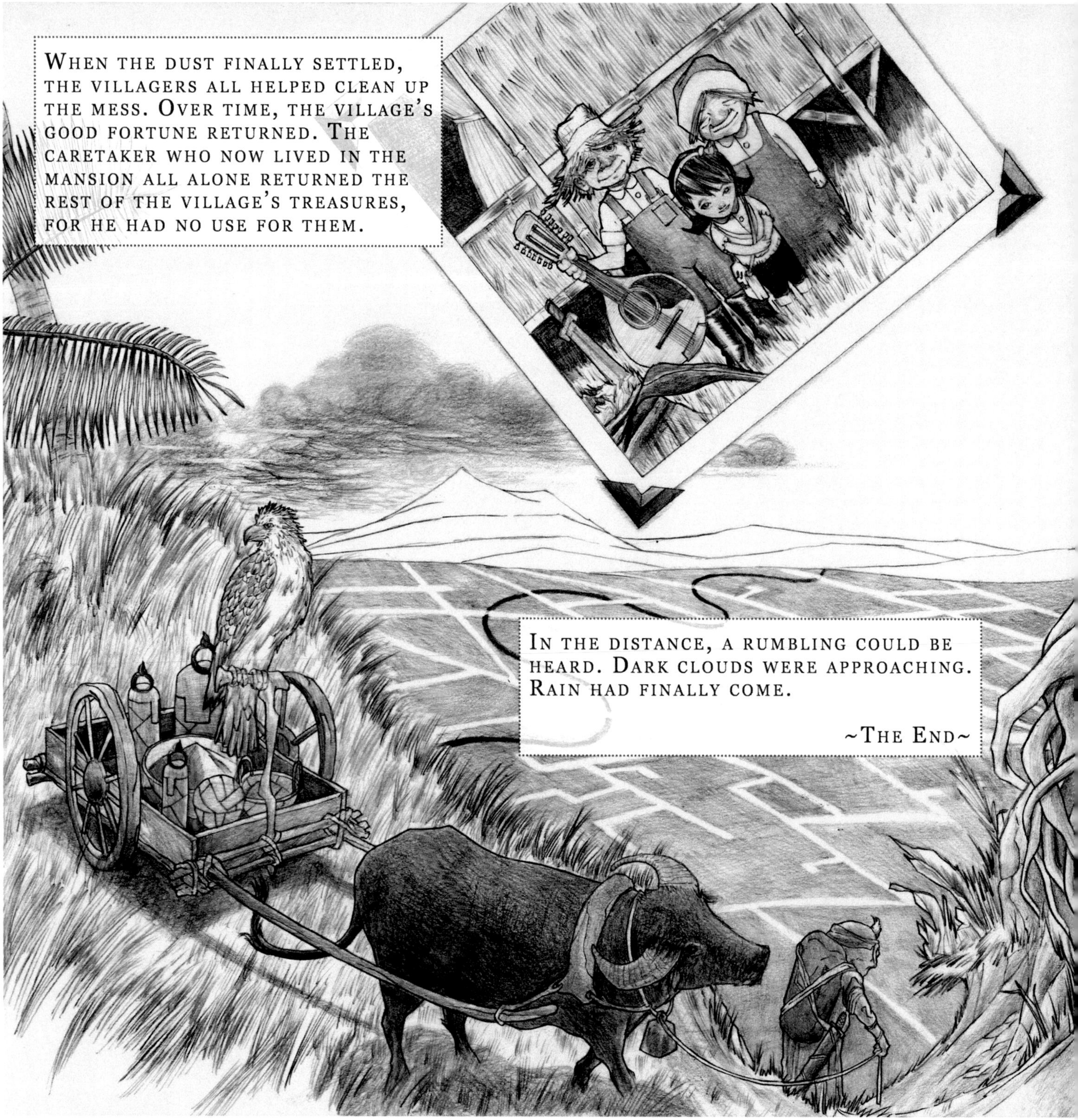

When the dust finally settled, the villagers all helped clean up the mess. Over time, the village's good fortune returned. The caretaker who now lived in the mansion all alone returned the rest of the village's treasures, for he had no use for them.

In the distance, a rumbling could be heard. Dark clouds were approaching. Rain had finally come.

~The End~

R. MARK YGONA HAS STUDIED
ART AND ARCHITECTURE FROM THE
UNIVERSITY OF WASHINGTON. HE
CURRENTLY LIVES WITH HIS FAMILY IN
ANN ARBOR, MI.

CONTACT INFO:
FEEDBACK4RMY@GMAIL.COM

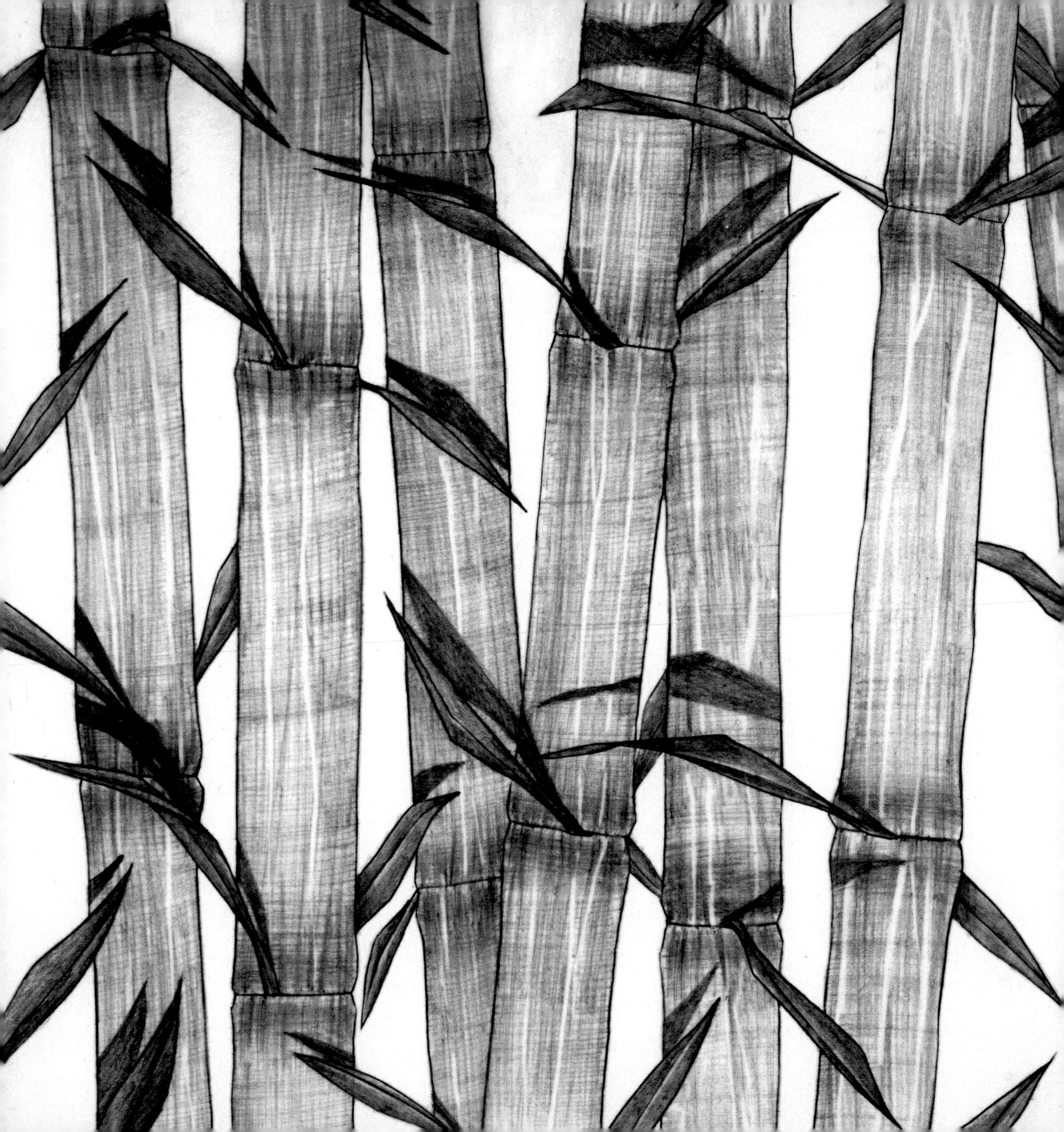